"THE OLD SWIMMIN'-HOLE" AND 'LEVEN MORE POEMS

NEGHBORLY POEMS

BY THE SAME AUTHOR

NEGHBORLY POEMS,
Including "the Old Swimmin' Hole."

SKETCHES IN PROSE,
Including the Boss Girl.

AFTERWHILES: Dialect
And Other Poetry.

PIPES O'PAN: Five Sketches
And Fifty Poems.

RHYMES OF CHILDHOOD: Dialect
And Other Verses.

PUBLISHED BY
THE BOWEN-MERRILL CO., INDIANAPOLIS.

IN ENGLAND—

OLD-FASHIONED ROSES:
Poems Dialect and Various.

PUBLISHED BY
LONGMANS, GREEN & CO., LONDON.

"THE OLD SWIMMIN'-HOLE" AND
'LEVEN MORE POEMS

NEGHBORLY POEMS

ON FRIENDSHIP
GRIEF AND
FARM-LIFE

BY

BENJ. F. JOHNSON, OF BOONE

[JAMES WHITCOMB RILEY.]

1891
THE BOWEN-MERRILL CO
INDIANAPOLIS, IND

DEDICATION

TO

THE EVER-FAITHFUL, WHOLE-SOULED, HONEST-HEARTED

HOOSIER FRIENDS, IN COUNTRY AND IN TOWN,

THIS LITTLE BOOK

IS GRATEFULLY AND LOVINGLY INSCRIBED.

PREFACE AND SUB-PREFACE.

As FAR back into boyhood as the writer's memory may intelligently go, the "country poet" is most pleasantly recalled. He was, and is, as common as the "country fiddler," and as full of good old-fashioned music. Not a master of melody, indeed, but a poet, certainly—

"Who, through long days of labor,
And nights devoid of ease,
Still heard in his soul the music
Of wonderful melodies."

And it is simply the purpose of this series of dialectic studies to reflect the real worth of this homely child of nature, and to echo faithfully, if possible, the faltering music of his song.

In adding to this series, as the writer has, for many years, been urged to do, and answering as steadfast a demand of Benj. F. Johnson's first and oldest friends, it has been decided that this further work of his be introduced to the reader of the volume as was the old man's first work to the reader of the newspaper of nearly ten years ago.

Directly, then, referring to the *Indianapolis*

Daily Journal—under whose management the writer had for some time been employed,—from issue of date June 17, 1882, under editorial caption of "A Boone County Pastoral," this article is herewith quoted:

Benj. F. Johnson, of Boone county, who considers the Journal a "very valubul" newspaper, writes to inclose us an original poem, desiring that we kindly accept it for publication, as "many neghbors and friends is astin' him to have the same struck off."

Mr. Johnson thoughtfully informs us that he is "no edjucated man," but that he has, "from childhood up tel old enugh to vote, allus wrote more er less poetry, as many of an albun in the neghborhood can testify." Again, he says that he writes "from the hart out;" and there is a touch of genuine pathos in the frank avowal, "Thare is times when I write the tears rolls down my cheeks."

In all sincerity, Mr. Johnson, we are glad to publish the poem you send, and just as you have written it. That is its greatest charm. Its very defects compose its excellence. You need no better education than the one from which emanates "The Old Swimmin'-Hole." It is real poetry, and all the more tender and lovable for the unquestionable evidence it bears of having been written "from the hart out." The only thing we find to—but hold! Let us first lay the poem before the reader:

Here followed the poem, "The Old Swimmin'-Hole," entire—the editorial comment ending as follows:

The only thing now, Mr. Johnson—as we were about to

observe—the only thing we find to criticise, at all relative to the poem, is your closing statement to the effect that "It was wrote to go to the tune of 'The Captin with his Whiskers!'" You should not have told us that, O Rare Ben. Johnson!

A week later, in the *Journal* of date June 24th, followed this additional mention of "Benj. F. Johnson, of Boone:"

It is a pleasure for us to note that the publication of the poem of "The Old Swimmin'-Hole," to which the Journal, with just pride, referred last week, has proved almost as great a pleasure to its author as to the hosts of delighted readers who have written in its praise, or called to personally indorse our high opinion of its poetic value. We have just received a letter from Mr. Johnson, the author, inclosing us another lyrical performance, which in many features even surpasses the originality and spirit of the former effort. Certainly the least that can be said of it is that it stands a thorough proof of our first assertion, that the author, though by no means a man of learning and profound literary attainments, is none the less a true poet and an artist. The letter, accompanying this later amaranth of blooming wildwood verse, we publish in its entirety, assured that Mr. Johnson's many admirers will be charmed, as we have been, at the delicious glimpse he gives us of his inspiration, modes of study, home-life and surroundings.

"To the Editer of the Indanoplus Jurnal:

"Respected Sir—The paper is here, markin' the old swimmin'-hole, my poetry which you seem to like so well. I joy to see it in print, and I thank you, hart and voice, for speakin' of its merrits in the way in which you do. I am glad you thought it was real poetry, as you said in your artikle. But I make bold to ast you what was your idy in sayin' I had ortent of told you it went to the tune I spoke of in my last. I felt highly flatered tel I got that fur. Was it because you don't know the tune refered to in the letter? Er wasent some words spelt right er not? Still ef you hadent of said somepin aginst it Ide of thought you was makin' fun. As I said before I well know my own unedjucation, but I don't think that is any reason the feelin's of the soul is stunted in theyr growth however. 'Juge not less ye be juged,' says The Good Book, and so say I, ef I thought you was makin' fun of the lines that I wrote and which you done me the onner to have printed off in sich fine style that I have read it over and over again in the paper you sent, and I would like to have about three more ef you can spare the same and state by mail what they will come at. All nature was in tune day before yisterday when your paper come to hand. It had ben a-raining hard fer some days, but that morning opened up as clear as a whissel. No clouds was in the sky, and the air was bammy with the warm sunshine and the wet smell of the earth and the locus blossoms and the flowrs and pennyroil and boneset. I got up, the first one about the place, and went forth to the plesant fields. I fed the stock with lavish hand and wortered them in merry glee, they was no bird in all the land no happier than me. I have jest wrote a verse of poetry in this letter; see ef you can find it. I also send you a whole poem which was wrote off the very day your paper come. I started it in the morning I have so feebly tride to pictur to you and wound her up by suppertime, besides doin' a fare day's work around the place.

Ef you print this one I think you will like it better than the other. This aint a sad poem like the other was, but you will find it full of careful thought. I pride myself on that. I also send you 30 cents in stamps fer you to take your pay out of fer the other papers I said, and also fer three more with this in it ef you have it printed and oblige. Ef you don't print this poem, keep the stamps and send me three more papers with *the other one* in—makin' the sum totul of six (6) papers altogether in full. Ever your true friend,

BENJ. F. JOHNSON.

"N. B.—The tune of this one is The Bold Privateer."

Here followed the poem, "Thoughts Fer The Discuraged Farmer;"—and here, too, fittingly ends any comment but that which would appear trivial and gratuitous.

Simply, in briefest conclusion, the hale, sound, artless, lovable character of Benj. F. Johnson remains, in the writer's mind, as from the first, far less a fiction than a living, breathing, vigorous reality.—So strong, indeed, has his personality been made manifest, that many times, in visionary argument with the sturdy old myth over certain changes from the original forms of his productions, he has so incontinently beaten down all suggestions as to a less incongruous association of thoughts and words, together with protests against his many violations of poetic method, harmony and grace, that nothing was left the writer but to submit to what has always seemed—and in truth still seems—a superior wisdom of dictation.

J. W. R.

Indianapolis, July 1891.

CONTENTS

"THE OLD SWIMMIN'-HOLE" AND 'LEVEN MORE POEMS

NEGHBORLY POEMS

THE DELIGHTS of our childhood is soon passed away,
And our gloryus youth it departs,—
And yit, dead and burried, they's blossoms of May
Ore theyr medderland graves in our harts.
So, friends of my barefooted days on the farm,
Whether truant in city er not,
God prosper you same as He's prosperin' me,
Whilse your past haint despised er fergot.

Oh! they's nothin', at morn, that's as grand unto me
As the glorys of Natchur so fare,—
With the Spring in the breeze, and the bloom in the trees,
And the hum of the bees ev'rywhare!
The green in the woods, and the birds in the boughs,
And the dew spangled over the fields;
And the bah of the sheep and the bawl of the cows
And the call from the house to your meals!

Then ho! fer your brekfast! and ho! fer the toil
That waiteth alike man and beast!
Oh! its soon with my team I'll be turnin' up soil,
Whilse the sun shoulders up in the East
Ore the tops of the ellums and beeches and oaks,
To smile his godspeed on the plow,
And the furry and seed, and the Man in his need,
And the joy of the swet of his brow!

"When I ust to lean above it on the old sickamore."

THE OLD SWIMMIN'-HOLE AND 'LEVEN MORE POEMS.

THE OLD SWIMMIN'-HOLE.

OH! the old swimmin'-hole! whare the crick so still and deep
Looked like a baby-river that was laying half asleep,
And the gurgle of the worter round the drift jest below
Sounded like the laugh of something we onc't ust to know
Before we could remember anything but the eyes
Of the angels lookin' out as we left Paradise;
But the merry days of youth is beyond our controle,
And it's hard to part ferever with the old swimmin'-hole.

Oh! the old swimmin'-hole! In the happy days of yore,
When I ust to lean above it on the old sickamore,
Oh! it showed me a face in its warm sunny tide
That gazed back at me so gay and glorified,
It made me love myself, as I leaped to caress
My shadder smilin' up at me with such tenderness.
But them days is past and gone, and old Time's tuck his toll
From the old man come back to the old swimmin'-hole.

Oh! the old swimmin'-hole! In the long, lazy days
When the hum-drum of school made so many run-a-ways,
How plesant was the jurney down the old dusty lane,
Whare the tracks of our bare feet was all printed so plane
You could tell by the dent of the heel and the sole
They was lots o' fun on hands at the old swimmin'-hole.
But the lost joys is past! Let your tears in sorrow roll
Like the rain that ust to dapple up the old swimmin'-hole.

Thare the bullrushes growed, and the cattails so tall,
And the sunshine and shadder fell over it all;
And it mottled the worter with amber and gold
Tel the glad lillies rocked in the ripples that rolled;
And the snake-feeder's four gauzy wings fluttered by
Like the ghost of a daisy dropped out of the sky,
Or a wownded apple-blossom in the breeze's controle
As it cut acrost some orchurd to'rds the old swimmin'-hole.

Oh! the old swimmin'-hole! When I last saw the place,
The scenes was all changed, like the change in my face;
The bridge of the railroad now crosses the spot
Whare the old divin'-log lays sunk and fergot.
And I stray down the banks whare the trees ust to be—
But never again will theyr shade shelter me!
And I wish in my sorrow I could strip to the soul,
And dive off in my grave like the old swimmin'-hole.

THOUGHTS FER THE DISCURAGED FARMER.

THE summer winds is sniffin' round the bloomin' locus' trees;
And the clover in the pastur' is a big day fer the bees,
And they been a-swiggin honey, above board and on the sly,
Tel they stutter in theyr buzzin' and stagger as they fly.
The flicker on the fence-rail 'pears to jest spit on his wings
And roll up his feathers, by the sassy way he sings;
And the hoss-fly is a-whettin'-up his forelegs fer biz,
And the off-mare is a-switchin' all of her tale they is.

You can hear the blackbirds jawin' as they foller up the plow—
Oh, theyr bound to git theyr brekfast, and theyr not a carin'
how;
So they quarrel in the furries, and they quarrel on the wing—
But theyr peaceabler in pot-pies than any other thing:
And its when I git my shotgun drawed up in stiddy rest,
She's as full of tribbelation as a yeller-jacket's nest;
And a few shots before dinner, when the sun's a-shinin' right,
Seems to kindo-sorto sharpen up a feller's appetite!

They's been a heap o' rain, but the sun's out to-day,
And the clouds of the wet spell is all cleared away,
And the woods is all the greener, and the grass is greener still;
It may rain again to-morry, but I don't think it will.

Some says the crops is ruined, and the corn's drownded out,
And propha-sy the wheat will be a failure, without doubt;
But the kind Providence that has never failed us yet,
Will be on hands onc't more at the 'leventh hour, I bet!

Does the medder-lark complane, as he swims high and dry
Through the waves of the wind and the blue of the sky?
Does the quail set up and whissel in a disappinted way,
Er hang his head in silunce, and sorrow all the day?
Is the chipmuck's health a-failin'? Does he walk, er does he run?
Don't the buzzards ooze around up thare jest like they've allus done?
Is they anything the matter with the rooster's lungs er voice?
Ort a mortul be complainin' when dumb animals rejoice?

Then let us, one and all, be contented with our lot;
The June is here this morning, and the sun is shining hot.
Oh! let us fill our harts up with the glory of the day,
And banish ev'ry doubt and care and sorrow fur away!
Whatever be our station, with Providence fer guide,
Sich fine circumstances ort to make us satisfied;
Fer the world is full of roses, and the roses full of dew,
And the dew is full of heavenly love that drips fer me and you.

A SUMMER'S DAY.

THE Summer's put the idy in
My head that I'm a boy again;
  And all around's so bright and gay
  I want to put my team away,
  And jest git out whare I can lay
  And soak my hide full of the day!
But work is work, and must be done—
Yit, as I work, I have my fun,
Jest fancyin' these furries here
Is childhood's paths onc't more so dear :—
And so I walk through medder-lands,
  And country lanes, and swampy trails
Whare long bullrushes bresh my hands;
  And, tilted on the ridered rails
    Of deadnin' fences, "Old Bob White"
    Whissels his name in high delight,
And whirrs away. I wunder still,
Whichever way a boy's feet will—
Whare trees has fell, with tangled tops
  Whare dead leaves shakes, I stop fer breth,
Heerin' the acorn as it drops—
  H'istin' my chin up still as deth,
And watchin' clos't, with upturned eyes,
The tree whare Mr. Squirrel tries
To hide hisse'f above the limb,
But lets his own tale tell on him.

I wunder on in deeper glooms—
  Git hungry, hearin' female cries
From old farm-houses, whare perfumes
  Of harvest dinners seems to rise
And ta'nt a feller, hart and brane,
With memories he can't explain.

I wunder through the underbresh,
  Whare pig-tracks, pintin' to'rds the crick
Is picked and printed in the fresh
  Black-bottom lands, like wimmern pick
Theyr pie-crusts with a fork, some way,
When bakin' fer camp-meetin' day.

I wunder on and on and on,
Tel my gray hair and beard is gone,
And ev'ry wrinkle on my brow
Is rubbed clean out and shaddered now
With curls as brown and fare and fine
As tenderls of the wild grape-vine
That ust to climb the highest tree
To keep the ripest ones fer me.
I wunder still, and here I am
Wadin' the ford below the dam—
The worter chucklin' round my knee
  At hornet-welt and bramble-scratch,
And me a-slippin' 'crost to see

Ef Tyner's plums is ripe, and size
The old man's wortermelon-patch,
With juicy mouth and drouthy eyes.
Then, after sich a day of mirth
And happiness as worlds is wurth—
So tired that heaven seems nigh about,—
The sweetest tiredness on earth
Is to git home and flatten out—
So tired you can't lay flat enugh,
And sort o' wish that you could spred
Out like molasses on the bed,
And jest drip off the aidges in
The dreams that never comes again.

A HYMB OF FAITH.

O, THOU that doth all things devise
  And fashon fer the best,
He'p us who sees with mortul eyes
  To overlook the rest.

They's times, of course, we grope in doubt,
  And in afflictions sore;
So knock the louder, Lord, without,
  And we'll unlock the door.

Make us to feel, when times looks bad
  And tears in pitty melts,
Thou wast the only he'p we had
  When they was nothin' else.

Death comes alike to ev'ry man
  That ever was borned on earth;
Then let us do the best we can
  To live fer all life's wurth.

Ef storms and tempusts dred to see
  Makes black the heavens ore,
They done the same in Galilee
  Two thousand years before.

But after all, the golden sun
  Poured out its floods on them
That watched and waited fer the One
  Then borned in Bethlyham.

Also, the star of holy writ
  Made noonday of the night,
Whilse other stars that looked at it
  Was envious with delight.

The sages then in wurship bowed,
  From ev'ry clime so fare;
O, sinner, think of that glad crowd
  That congergated thare!

They was content to fall in ranks
  With One that knowed the way
From good old Jurden's stormy banks
  Clean up to Jedgmunt Day.

No matter, then, how all is mixed
  In our near-sighted eyes,
All things is fer the best, and fixed
  Out straight in Paradise.

Then take things as God sends 'em here,
  And, ef we live er die,
Be more and more contenteder,
  Without a-astin' why.

O, thou that doth all things devise
  And fashon fer the best,
He'p us who sees with mortul eyes.
  To overlook the rest.

WORTER-MELON TIME.

OLD worter-melon time is a-comin'round again,
And they ain't no man a-livin' any tickleder'n me,
Fer the way I hanker after worter-melons is a sin—
Which is the why and wharefore, as you can plainly see.

Oh! it's in the sandy soil worter-melons does the best,
And its thare they'll lay and waller in the sunshine and the dew
Till they wear all the green streaks clean off of theyr breast;
And you bet I ain't a-findin' any fault with them; air you?

They ain't no better thing in the vegetable line;
And they don't need much 'tendin', as ev'ry farmer knows;
And when theyr ripe and ready fer to pluck from the vine,
I want to say to you theyr the best fruit that grows.

It's some likes the yeller-core, and some likes the red,
And it's some says "The little Californy" is the best;
But the sweetest slice of all I ever wedged in my head,
Is the old "Edingburg Mounting-sprout," of the west.

You don't want no punkins nigh your worter-melon vines—
'Cause, some-way-another, they'll spile your melons, shore;—
I've seed 'em taste like punkins, from the core to the rines,
Which may be a fact you have heered of before.

But your melons that's raised right and 'tended to with care,
You can walk around amongst 'em with a parent's pride and joy,
And thump 'em on the heads with as fatherly a air
As ef each one of them was your little girl er boy.

I joy in my hart jest to hear that rippin' sound
When you split one down the back and jolt the halves in two,
And the friends you love the best is gethered all around—
And you says unto your sweethart, "Oh here's the core fer you!"

And I like to slice 'em up in big pieces fer 'em all,
Espeshally the childern, and watch theyr high delight
As one by one the rines with theyr pink notches falls,
And they holler fer some more, with unquenched appetite.

Boys takes to it natchurl, and I like to see 'em eat—
A slice of worter-melon's like a frenchharp in theyr hands,
And when they "saw" it through theyr mouth sich music can't be beat—
'Cause it's music both the sperit and the stummick under-stands.

Oh, they's more in worter-melons than the purty-colored meat,
And the overflowin' sweetness of the worter squshed be-twixt

The up'ard and the down'ard motions of a feller's teeth,
  And it's the taste of ripe old age and juicy childhood mixed.

Fer I never taste a melon but my thoughts flies away
  To the summertime of youth; and again I see the dawn,
And the fadin' afternoon of the long summer day,
  And the dusk and dew a-fallin', and the night a-comin' on.

And thare's the corn around us, and the lispin' leaves and trees,
  And the stars a-peekin' down on us as still as silver mice,
And us boys in the worter-melons on our hands and knees,
  And the new-moon hangin' ore us like a yeller-cored slice.

Oh! it's worter-melon time is a-comin' round again,
  And they ain't no man a-livin' any tickleder'n me,
Fer the way I hanker after worter-melons is a sin—
  Which is the why and wharefore, as you can plainly see.

MY PHILOSOFY.

I AINT, ner don't p'tend to be,
Much posted on philosofy;
But thare is times, when all alone,
I work out idees of my own.
And of these same thare is a few
I'd like to jest refer to you—
Pervidin' that you don't object
To listen clos't and rickollect.

I allus argy that a man
Who does about the best he can
Is plenty good enugh to suit
This lower mundane institute—
No matter ef his daily walk
Is subject fer his neghbor's talk,
And critic-minds of ev'ry whim
Jest all git up and go fer him!

I knowed a feller onc't that had
The yeller-janders mighty bad,
And each and ev'ry friend he'd meet
Would stop and give him some receet
Fer cuorin' of 'em. But he'd say
He kind o' thought they'd go away
Without no medicin', and boast
That he'd git well without one doste.

He kep' a yellerin' on—and they
Perdictin' that he'd die some day
Before he knowed it! Tuck his bed,
The feller did, and lost his head,
And wundered in his mind a spell—
Then rallied, and, at last, got well;
But ev'ry friend that said he'd die
Went back on him eternally!

Its natchurl enugh, I guess,
When some gits more and some gits less,
Fer them-uns on the slimmest side
To claim it ain't a fare divide;
And I've knowed some to lay and wait,
And git up soon, and set up late,
To ketch some feller they could hate
Fer goin' at a faster gait.

The signs is bad when folks commence
A findin' fault with Providence,
And balkin' 'cause the earth don't shake
At ev'ry prancin' step they take.
No man is great tel he can see
How less than little he would be
Ef stripped to self, and stark and bare
He hung his sign out anywhare.

My doctern is to lay aside
Contensions, and be satisfied:
Jest do your best, and praise er blame
That follers that, counts jest the same.
I've allus noticed grate success
Is mixed with troubles, more er less,
And its the man who does the best
That gits more kicks than all the rest.

WHEN THE FROST IS ON THE PUNKIN.

WHEN the frost is on the punkin and the fodder's in the shock,
And you hear the kyouck and gobble of the struttin' turkey-cock,
And the clackin'of the guineys, and the cluckin' of the hens,
And the rooster's hallylooyer as he tiptoes on the fence;
O its then's the times a feller is a-feelin' at his best,
With the risin' sun to greet him from a night of peaceful rest,
As he leaves the house, bare-headed, and goes out to feed the stock,
When the frost is on the punkin and the fodder's in the shock.

They's something kindo' harty-like about the atmosfere
When the heat of summer's over and the coolin' fall is here—
Of course we miss the flowers, and the blossoms on the trees,
And the mumble of the hummin'-birds and buzzin' of the bees;
But the air's so appetizin'; and the landscape through the haze
Of a crisp and sunny morning of the airly autumn days
Is a pictur' that no painter has the colorin' to mock—
When the frost is on the punkin and the fodder's in the shock.

"When the frost is on the punkin and the fodder's in the shock."

The husky, rusty russel of the tossels of the corn,
And the raspin of the tangled leaves, as golden as the morn;
The stubble in the furries—kindo' lonesome-like, but still
A-preachin' sermuns to us of the barns they growed to fill;
The strawstack in the medder, and the reaper in the shed;
The hosses in theyr stalls below—the clover overhead!—
O, it sets my hart a-clickin' like the tickin' of a clock,
When the frost is on the punkin and the fodder's in the shock!

Then your apples all is getherd, and the ones a feller keeps
Is poured around the celler-floor in red and yeller heaps;
And your cider-makin's over, and your wimmern-folks is through
With their mince and apple buttcr, and theyr souse and saussage, too;—
I don't know how to tell it—but ef sich a thing could be
As the Angels wantin' boardin', and they'd call around on *me*—
I'd want to 'commodate 'em—all the whole-indurin' flock,
When the frost is on the punkin and the fodder's in the shock!

ON THE DEATH OF LITTLE MAHALA ASHCRAFT.

"LITTLE HALY! Little Haly!" cheeps the robin in the tree;
"Little Haly!" sighs the clover, "Little Haly!" moans the bee;
"Little Haly! Little Haly!" calls the kill-deer at twilight;
And the katydids and crickets hollers "Haly" all the night.

The sunflowers and the hollyhawks droops over the garden fence;
The old path down the gardenwalks still holds her footprints' dents;
And the well-sweep's swingin' bucket seems to wait fer her to come
And start it on its wortery errant down the old bee-gum.

The bee-hives all is quiet, and the little Jersey steer,
When any one comes nigh it, acts so lonesome like and queer;
And the little Banty chickens kind o' cutters faint and low,
Like the hand that now was feedin' 'em was one they didn't know.

They's sorrow in the wavin' leaves of all the apple-trees;
And sorrow in the harvest-sheaves, and sorrow in the breeze;
And sorrow in the twitter of the swallers 'round the shed;
And all the song her red-bird sings is "Little Haly's dead!"

The medder 'pears to miss her, and the pathway through the
  grass,
Whare the dewdrops ust to kiss her little bare feet as she
  passed;
And the old pin in the gate-post seems to kindo-sorto' doubt
That Haly's little sunburnt hands'll ever pull it out.

Did her father er her mother ever love her more'n me,
Er her sisters er her brother prize her love more tendurly?
I question—and what answer?—only tears, and tears alone,
And ev'ry neghbor's eyes is full o' tear-drops as my own.

"Little Haly! Little Haly!" cheeps the robin in the tree;
"Little Haly!" sighs the clover, "Little Haly!" moans the bee;
"Little Haly! Little Haly!" calls the kill-deer at twilight,
And the katydids and crickets hollers "Haly" all the night.

THE MULBERRY TREE.

O, ITS many's the scenes which is dear to my mind
As I think of my childhood so long left behind;
The home of my birth, with its old puncheon-floor,
And the bright morning-glorys that growed round the door;
The warped clab-board roof whare the rain it run off
Into streams of sweet dreams as I laid in the loft,
Countin' all of the joys that was dearest to me,
And a-thinkin' the most of the mulberry tree.

And to-day as I dream, with both eyes wide-awake,
I can see the old tree, and its limbs as they shake,
And the long purple berries that rained on the ground
Whare the pastur' was bald whare we trommpt it around.
And again, peekin' up through the thick leafy shade,
I can see the glad smiles of the friends when I strayed
With my little bare feet from my own mother's knee
To foller them off to the mulberry tree.

Leanin' up in the forks, I can see the old rail,
And the boy climbin' up it, claw, tooth, and toe-nail,
And in fancy can hear, as he spits on his hands,
The ring of his laugh and the rip of his pants.
But that rail led to glory, as certin and shore
As I'll never climb thare by that rout' any more—
What was all the green lauruls of Fame unto me,
With my brows in the boughs of the mulberry tree!

Then its who can fergit the old mulberry tree
That he knowed in the days when his thoughts was as free
As the flutterin' wings of the birds that flew out
Of the tall wavin' tops as the boys come about?
O, a crowd of my memories, laughin' and gay,
Is a-climbin' the fence of that pastur' to-day,
And a-pantin' with joy, as us boys ust to be,
They go racin' acrost fer the mulberry tree.

TO MY OLD FRIEND, WILLIAM LEACHMAN.

FER forty year and better you have been a friend to me,
Through days of sore afflictions and dire adversity,
You allus had a kind word of counsul to impart,
Which was like a healin' 'intment to the sorrow of my hart.

When I burried my first womern, William Leachman, it was you
Had the only consolation that I could listen to—
Fer I knowed you had gone through it and had rallied from the blow,
And when you said I'd do the same, I knowed you'd ort to know.

But that time I'll long remember; how I wundered here and thare—
Through the settin'-room and kitchen, and out in the open air—
And the snowflakes whirlin', whirlin', and the fields a frozen glare,
And the neghbors' sleds and wagons congergatin' ev'rywhare.

I turned my eyes to'rds heaven, but the sun was hid away;
I turned my eyes to'rds earth again, but all was cold and gray;
And the clock, like ice a-crackin', clickt the icy hours in two—
And my eyes'd never thawed out ef it hadn't been fer you!

We set thare by the smoke-house—me and you out thare
alone—
Me a-thinkin'—you a-talkin' in a soothin' undertone—
You a-talkin'—me a-thinkin' of the summers long ago,
And a-writin' "Marthy—Marthy" with my finger in the snow!

William Leachman, I can see jest as plane as I could then;
And your hand is on my shoulder, and you rouse me up again;
And I see the tears a-drippin' from your own eyes, as you say:
"Be rickonciled and bear it—we but linger fer a day!"

At the last Old Settlers' Meetin' we went j'intly, you and
me—
Your hosses and my wagon, as you wanted it to be;
And sence I can remember, from the time we've neghbored
here,
In all sich friendly actions you have double-done your sheer.

It was better than the meetin', too, that 9-mile talk we had
Of the times when we first settled here and travel was so bad;
When we had to go on hoss-back, and sometimes on "Shanks's
mare,"
And "blaze" a road fer them behind that had to travel thare.

And now we was a-trottin' 'long a level gravel pike,
In a big two-hoss road-wagon, jest as easy as you like—
Two of us on the front seat, and our wimmern-folks behind,
A-settin' in theyr Winsor cheers in perfect peace of mind!

And we pinted out old landmarks, nearly faded out of sight:—
Thare they ust to rob the stage-coach; thare Gash Morgan had the fight
With the old stag-deer that pronged him—how he battled fer his life,
And lived to prove the story by the handle of his knife.

Thare the first griss-mill was put up in the Settlement, and we
Had tuck our grindin' to it in the Fall of Forty-three—
When we tuck our rifles with us, techin' elbows all the way,
And a-stickin' right together ev'ry minute, night and day.

Thare ust to stand the tavern that they called the "Travelers' Rest,"
And thare, beyent the covered bridge, "The Counterfitters' Nest"—
Whare they claimed the house was ha'nted—that a man was murdered thare,
And burried underneath the floor, er 'round the place somewhare.

And the old Plank-road they laid along in Fifty-one er two—
You know we talked about the times when the old road was new:
How "Uncle Sam" put down that road and never taxed the State
Was a problum, don't you rickollect, we couldn't dimonstrate?

And thare, beyent the covered bridge, "The Counterfitters' Nest."

Ways was devius, William Leachman, that me and you has past;
But as I found you true at first, I find you true at last;
And, now the time's a-comin' mighty nigh our jurney's end,
I want to throw wide open all my soul to you, my friend.

With the stren'th of all my bein', and the heat of hart and brane,
And ev'ry livin' drop of blood in artery and vane,
I love you and respect you, and I venerate your name,
Fer the name of William Leachman and True Manhood's jest the same!

MY FIDDLE.

My fiddle?—Well, I kindo' keep her handy, don't you know!
Though I aint so much inclined to tromp the strings and switch the bow
As I was before the timber of my elbows got so dry,
And my fingers was more limber-like and caperish and spry;
Yit I can plonk and plunk and plink,
And tune her up and play,
And jest lean back and laugh and wink
At ev'ry rainy day!

My playin's only middlin'—tunes I picked up when a boy—
The kindo'-sorto' fiddlin' that the folks calls "cordaroy;"
"The Old Fat Gal," and "Rye-straw," and "My Sailyor's on the Sea,"
Is the old cowtillions *I* "saw" when the ch'ice is left to me;
And so I plunk and plonk and plink,
And rosum-up my bow,
And play the tunes that makes you think
The devil's in your toe!

I was allus a romancin', do-less boy, to tell the truth,
A-fiddlin' and a-dancin', and a-wastin' of my youth,
And a-actin' and a-cuttin'-up all sorts o' silly pranks
That wasn't worth a button of anybody's thanks!
But they tell me, when I ust to plink
And plonk and plunk and play,
My music seemed to have the kink
O' drivin' cares away!

That's how this here old fiddle's won my hart's indurin love!
From the strings acrost her middle, to the schreechin' keys above—
From her "apern," over "bridge," and to the ribbon round her throat,
She's a wooin', cooin' pigeon, singin' "Love me" ev'ry note!
And so I pat her neck, and plink
Her strings with lovin' hands,
And, list'nin' clos't, I sometimes think
She kindo' understands!

THE CLOVER.

SOME sings of the lilly, and daisy, and rose,
And the pansies and pinks that the Summertime throws
In the green grassy lap of the medder that lays
Blinkin' up at the skyes through the sunshiney days;
But what is the lilly and all of the rest
Of the flowers, to a man with a hart in his brest
That was dipped brimmin' full of the honey and dew
Of the sweet clover-blossoms his babyhood knew?

I never set eyes on a clover-field now,
Er fool round a stable, er climb in the mow,
But my childhood comes back jest as clear and as plane
As the smell of the clover I'm sniffin' again;
And I wunder away in a bare-footed dream,
Whare I tangle my toes in the blossoms that gleam
With the dew of the dawn of the morning of love
Ere it wept ore the graves that I'm weepin' above.

And so I love clover—it seems like a part
Of the sacerdest sorrows and joys of my hart;
And wharever it blossoms, oh, thare let me bow
And thank the good God as I'm thankin' Him now;
And I pray to Him still fer the stren'th when I die,
To go out in the clover and tell it good-bye,
And lovin'ly nestle my face in its bloom
While my soul slips away on a breth of purfume.

NEGHBORLY POEMS

ON FRIENDSHIP, GRIEF AND FARM-LIFE

✓

US FARMERS in the country, as the seasons go and come,
Is purty much like other folks,—we're apt to grumble some!
The Spring's too back'ard fer us, er too for'ard—ary one—
We'll jaw about it anyhow, and have our way er none!
The thaw's set in too suddent; er the frost's stayed in the soil
Too long to give the wheat a chance, and crops is bound to spoil!
The weather's either most too mild, er too outrageous rough,
And altogether too much rain, er not half rain enugh!

Now what I'd like and what you'd like is plane enugh to see:
Its jest to have old Providence drop round on you and me
And ast us what our views is first, regardin' shine er rain,
And post 'em when to shet her off, er let her on again!
And yit I'd ruther, after all—considern other chores
I' got on hands, a'-tendin' both to my affairs and yours—
I'd ruther miss the blame I'd git, a-rulin' things up thare,
And spend my extry time in praise and gratitude and prayer.

ERASMUS WILSON.

'RAS WILSON, I respect you, 'cause
You're common, like you allus was
Afore you went to town and s'prised
The world by gittin' "reckonized,"
And yit perservin, as I say,
Your common hoss-sense ev'ryway!
And when that name o' yourn occurs
On hand-bills, er in newspapers,
Er letters writ by friends 'at ast
About you, same as in the past,
And neghbors and relations 'low
You're out o' the tall timber now,
And "gittin' thare" about as spry's
The next!—as *I say*, when my eyes,
Er ears, lights on your name, I mind
The first time'at I come to find
You—and my Rickollection yells,
Jest jubilunt as old sleigh-bells—
"'Ras Wilson! Say! Hold up! and shake
A paw, fer old acquaintance sake!"

My *Rickollection*, more'n like,
Haint overly too apt to strike
That what's-called cultchurd public eye
As wisdum of the deepest dye,—
And yit my Rickollection makes
So blame lots fewer bad mistakes,
Regardin' human-natchur' and
The fellers 'at I've shook theyr hand,
Than my *best jedgemunt's* done, the day
I've met 'em—'fore I got away,—
'At—Well, 'Ras Wilson, let me grip
Your hand in warmest pardnership!

Dad-burn ye!—Like to jest haul back
A' old flat-hander, jest che-whack!
And take you 'twixt the shoulders, say,
Sometime you're lookin' t'other way!—
Er, maybe whilse you're speakin' to
A whole blame Courthouse-full o' 'thu-
Syastic friends, I'd like to jest
Come in-like and break up the nest
Afore you hatched anuther cheer,
And say: " 'Ras, *I* can't stand hitched here
All night—ner wouldn't ef I could!—
But Little Bethel neghborhood,
You ust to live at, 's sent some word
Fer you, ef ary chance occurred

To git it to ye,—so ef you
Kin stop, I'm waitin' fer ye to!"

You're common as I said afore—
You're common, yit uncommon *more.*—
You allus kindo' 'pear, to me,
What all mankind had ort to be—
Jest *natchurl,* and the more hurraws
You git, the less you know the cause—
Like as ef God Hisself stood by,
Where best on earth hain't half knee-high,
And seein' like, and' knowin' He
'S the Only Great Man really,
You're jest content to size your hight
With any feller-man's in sight.—
And even then they's scrubs, like me,
Feels stuck-up, in your company!

Like now:—I want to go with you
Plum out o' town a mile er two
Clean past the Fair-ground whare's some hint
O' pennyrile er peppermint,
And bottom-lands, and timber thick
Enugh to sorto' shade the crick!
I want to *see* you—want to set
Down somers, whare the grass hain't wet,

And kindo' *breathe* you, like puore air—
And taste o' your tobacker thare,
And talk and chaw! Talk o' the birds
We've knocked with cross-bows.—Afterwards
Drop, mayby, into some dispute
'Bout "pomgrannies," er cal'mus-root—
And how *they* growed, and *whare?*—on tree
Er vine?—Who's best boy-memory!—
And wasn't it gingsang, insted
O' Cal'mus-root, growed like you said?—
Er how to tell a coon-track from
A mussrat's;—er how milksick come—
Er ef *cows* brung it?—Er why now
We never see no "muley"-cow—
Ner "frizzly"-chicken—ner no "clay-
Bank" mare—ner nothin' thataway!—
And what's come o' the yeller-core
Old wortermelons?—hain't no more.—
Tomattusus, the same—all red-
Uns nowadays—All past joys fled—
Each and all jest gone k-whizz!
Like our days o' childhood is!

Dag-gone it, Ras! they hain't no friend,
It 'pears-like, left to comperhend
Sich things as these but you, and see
How dratted sweet they air to me!

But you, 'at's loved 'em allus, and
Kin sort 'em out and understand
'Em, same as the fine books you've read,
And all fine thoughts you've writ, er said,
Er worked out, through long nights o' rain,
And doubts and fears, and hopes, again,
As bright as morning when she broke,—
You know a teardrop from a joke!
  And so, 'Ras Wilson, stop and shake
  A paw, fer old acquaintance sake!

MY RUTHERS.

[Writ durin' State Fair at Indanoplis, whilse visitin' a Soninlaw then residin' thare, who has sence got back to the country whare he says a man that's raised thare ort to a-stayed in the first place.]

I tell you what I'd ruther do—
Ef I only had my ruthers,—
I'd ruther work when I wanted to
Than be bossed round by others;—
I'd ruther kindo' git the swing
O' what was *needed*, first, I jing!
Afore I *swet* at anything!—
Ef I only had my ruthers;—
In fact I'd aim to be the same
With all men as my brothers;
And they'd all be the same with *me*—
Ef I only had my ruthers.

I wouldn't likely know it all—
Ef I only had my ruthers;—
I'd know *some* sense, and some base-ball—
Some *old* jokes, and—some others:
I'd know *some politics*, and 'low
Some tarif-speeches same as now,
Then go hear Nye on "Branes and How
To Detect Theyr Presence." *T'others*,
That stayed away, I'd *let* 'em stay—
All my dissentin' brothers

Could chuse as shore a kill er cuore,
  Ef I only had my ruthers.

The pore 'ud git theyr dues *some*times—
  Ef I only had my ruthers,—
And be paid *dollars* 'stid o' *dimes*,
  Fer childern, wives and mothers:
    Theyr boy that slaves; theyr girl that sews—
    Fer *others*—not herself, God knows!—
    The grave's *her* only change of clothes!
  ...Ef I only had my ruthers,
They'd all have "stuff" and time enugh
  To answer one-another's
Appealin' prayer fer "lovin' care"—
  Ef I only had my ruthers.

They'd be few folks 'ud ast fer trust,
  Ef I only had my ruthers,
And blame few business-men to bu'st
  Theyrselves, er harts of others:
    Big Guns that come here durin' Fair-
    Week could put up jest anywhare,
    And find a full-and-plenty thare,
  Ef I only had my ruthers:
The rich and great 'ud 'sociate
  With all theyr lowly brothers,
Feelin' *we* done the honorun—
  Ef I only had my ruthers.

ON A DEAD BABE.

FLY away! thou heavenly one!—
I do hail thee on thy flight!
Sorrow? thou hath tasted none—
Perfect joy is yourn by right.
Fly away! and bear our love
To thy kith and kin above!

I can tetch thy finger-tips
Ca'mly, and bresh back the hair
From thy forr'ed with my lips,
And not leave a teardrop thare.—
Weep fer *Tomps and Ruth*—and *me*—
But I cannot weep fer *thee.*

A OLD PLAYED-OUT SONG.

IT'S THE curiousest thing in creation,
  Whenever I hear that old song,
"Do They Miss Me at Home," I'm so bothered,
  My life seems as short as it's long!—
Fer ev'rything 'pears like adzackly
  It 'peared in the years past and gone,—
When I started out sparkin' at twenty,
  And had my first neckercher on!

Though I'm wrinkelder, older and grayer
  Right now than my parents was then,
You strike up that song, "Do They Miss Me,"
  And I'm jest a youngster again!—
I'm a-standin' back thare in the furries
  A-wishin' fer evening to come,
And a-whisperin' over and over
  Them words, "Do They Miss Me at Home?"

You see, *Marthy Ellen she* sung it
  The first time I heerd it; and so,
As she was my very first sweethart,
  It reminds me of her, don't you know;—

How her face ust to look, in the twilight,
As I tuck her to Spellin'; and she
Kep' a-hummin' that song tel I ast her,
Pine-blank, ef she ever missed *me*!

I can shet my eyes now, as you sing it,
And hear her low answerin' words;
And then the glad chirp of the crickets,
As clear as the twitter of birds;
And the dust in the road is like velvet,
And the ragweed and fennel and grass
Is as sweet as the scent of the lillies
Of Eden of old, as we pass.

"*Do They Miss Me at Home?*" Sing it lower—
And softer—and sweet as the breeze
That powdered our path with the snowy
White bloom of the old locus'-trees!
Let the whipperwills he'p you to sing it,
And the echoes 'way over the hill,
Tel the moon boolges out, in a chorus
Of stars, and our voices is still.

But, oh! "They's a chord in the music
That's missed when *her* voice is away!"
Though I listen from midnight tel morning,
And dawn tel the dusk of the day!

And I grope through the dark, lookin' up'ards
  And on through the heavenly dome,
With my longin' soul singin' and sobbin'
  The words, "Do They Miss Me at Home?"

"COON-DOG WESS."

"Coon-dog Wess"—he allus went
  'Mongst us here by that-air name.
Moved in this-here Settlement
  From next county—he laid claim,—
Lived down in the bottoms—whare
Ust to be some coons in thare!—

In nigh Clayton's, next the crick,—
  Mind old Billy ust to say
Coons in thare was jest that thick,
  He'p him corn-plant any day!—
And, in rostneer-time, be then
Aggin' him to plant again!

Well,—In Spring o' '67,
  This-here "Coon-dog Wess" he come—
Fetchin' 'long 'bout forty-'leven
  Ornriest-lookin' hounds, I gum!
Ever mortul-man laid eyes
On sence dawn o' Christian skies!

Wife come traipsin' at the rag-
  Tag-and-bobtail of the crowd,
Dogs and childern, with a bag
  Corn-meal and some side-meat,—*Proud*
And as *independunt—My!*—
Yit a mild look in her eye.

Well—this "Coon-dog Wess" he jest
  Moved in that-air little pen
Of a pole-shed, aidgin' west
  On "The Slues o' Death," called then.—
Otter and mink-hunters ust
To camp thare 'fore game vam-moosd.

Abul-bodied man,—and lots
  Call fer *choppers*—and fer hands
To git *cross-ties* out.—But what's
  Work to sich as understands
Ways appinted and is hence
Under special providence?—

"Coon-dog Wess's" holts was *hounds*
  And *coon-huntin'*; and he knowed
His own range, and stayed in bounds,
  And left work fer them 'at showed
Talents fer it—same as his
Gifts regardin' coon-dogs is.

Hounds of ev'ry mungerl breed
  Ever whelped on earth!—Had these
Yeller kind, with punkin-seed
  Marks above theyr eyes—and fleas
Both to sell and keep!—Also
These-here lop-yeerd hounds, you know.—

Yes-and *brindle* hounds—and long,
  Ga'nt hounds, with them eyes they' got
So blame *sorry*, it seems wrong,
  'Most, to kick 'em as to not!
Man, though, wouldn't dast, I guess,
Kick a hound fer coon-dog Wess!"

'Tended to his own affairs
  Stric'ly;--made no brags,—and yit
You could see 'at them hounds' cares
  'Peared like *his*,—and he'd a-fit
Fer 'em, same as wife er child!—
Them facts made folks rickonciled,

Sorto', fer to let him be
  And not pester him. And then
Word begin to spread 'at he
  Had brung in as high as ten
Coon-pelts in one night—and yit
Didn't 'pear to boast of it!

Neghborhood made some complaints
'Bout them plague-gone hounds at night
Howlin' fit to wake the saints,
Clean from dusk tel plum day-light!
But to "Coon-dog Wess" them-thare
Howls was "music in the air!"

Fetched his pelts to Gilson's Store—
Newt he shipped fer him, and said,
Sence *he'd* cooned thare, he'd shipped more
Than three hunderd pelts!—"By Ned!
Git shet of my store," Newt says,
"I'd go in with 'Coon-dog Wess'!"

And the feller 'peared to be
Makin' best and most he could
Of his rale prospairity:—
Bought some household things—and *good*,—
Likewise, wagon-load onc't come
From wharever he'd moved from.

But pore feller's huntin'-days,
'Bout them times, was glidin' past!—
Goes out onc't one night and *stays!*
...Neghbors they turned out, at last,
Headed by his wife and one
Half-starved hound—and search begun.

Boys said, that blame hound, he led
  Searchin' party, 'bout a half
Mile ahead, and bellerin', said,
  Worse'n ary yearlin' calf!—
Tel, at last, come fur-off sounds
Like the howl of other hounds.

And-sir, shore enugh, them signs
  Fetched 'em—in a' hour er two—
Whare the *pack* was;—and they finds
  "Coon-dog Wess" *right thare;*—And you
Would admitted he was right
Stayin', as he had, *all night!*

Facts is, cuttin' down a tree,
  The blame thing had sorto' fell
In a twist-like—*mercy me!*
  And had ketched him.—Couldn't tell,
Wess said, *how* he'd managed—yit
He'd got both legs under it!

Fainted and come to, I s'pose,
  'Bout a dozen times whilse they
Chopped him out!—And wife she froze
  To him!—bresh his hair away
And smile cheerful'—only when
He'd faint.—Cry and kiss him *then.*

Had *his* nerve!—And nussed him through,—
  Neghbors he'pped her—all she'd stand.—
Had a loom, and she could do
  Carpet-weavin' railly grand!—
"'Sides," she ust to laugh and say,
"She'd have Wess, now, night and day!"

As fer *him*, he'd say, says-ee,
  "I'm resigned to bein' lame:—
They was four coons up that tree,
  And hounds got 'em, jest the same!"
'Peared like, one er two legs less
Never worried "Coon-dog Wess!"

LINES TO
PERFESSER JOHN CLARK RIDPATH A. M., LL. D. T-Y-TY!

[Cumposed by A Old Friend of the Fambily sence 'way back in the Forties, when they Settled nigh Fillmore, Putnum County, this State, whare John was borned and growed up, you might say, like the wayside flower.]

YOUR neghbors in the country, whare you come from, haint fergot!—
We knowed you even better than your own-self, like as not.
We profissied your runnin'-geers 'ud stand a soggy load
And pull her, purty stiddy, up a mighty rocky road:
We been a-watchin your career sence you could write your name—
But way you writ it *first*, I'll say, was jest a burnin' shame!—
Your "J. C." in the copybook, and "Ridpath"—mercy-sakes!—
Quiled up and tide in dubble bows, lookt like a nest o' snakes!—
But *you* could read it, I *suppose*, and kindo' gloted on
A-bein' "*J. C. Ridpath*" when we only called you "John."

But you'd work 's well as fool, and what you had to do was *done:*
We've watched you at the woodpile—not the *woodshed*—wasent none,—

And snow and sleet, and haulin', too, and lookin' after stock,
And milkin', nights, and feedin' pigs,—then turnin' back the clock,
So's you could set up studyin' your 'Rethmatic, and fool
Your Parents, whilse a-piratin' your way through winter school!
And I've heerd tell—from your own folks—you've set and baked your face
A-readin' Plutark Slives all night by that old fi-er-place.—
Yit, 'bout them times, the blackboard, onc't, had on it, I *de*-clare,
"Yours truly, *J. Clark* Ridpath,"—and the teacher—left it thare!

And they was other symptums, too, that pinted, plane as day
To nothin' short of *College!*—and *one* was the lovin' way
Your mother had of cheerin' you to efforts brave and strong,
And puttin' more faith in you, as you needed it along;
She'd pat you on the shoulder, er she'd grab you by the hands,
And laugh sometimes, er cry sometimes.—They's few that understands
Jest what theyr mother's drivin' at when they act thataway;—
But I'll say this fer *you*, John-Clark,—you answered, night and day,
To ev'ry trust and hope of hers—and half your College fame
Was battled fer and won fer her and glory of her name.

The likes of *you* at *College!* But you went there. How you paid
Your way nobody's astin'—but you *worked*,—you haint afraid,—
Your *clothes* was, more'n likely, kindo' out o' style, perhaps,
And not as snug and warm as some 'at hid the other chaps;—
But when it come to *Intullect*—they tell me yourn was dressed
A *leetle* mite *superber*, like, than any of the rest!
And thare you *stayed*—and thare you've made your rickord, fare and square—
Tel *now* its *Fame* 'at writes your name, approvin', *ev'rywhare*—
Not *jibblets* of it, nuther,—but all John Clark Ridpath, set
Plum 'at the dashboard of the whole-endurin' Alphabet!

A TALE OF THE AIRLY DAYS.

OH! tell me a tale of the airly days—
  Of the times as they ust to be;
"Piller of Fi-er" and "Shakspeare's Plays"
  Is a' most too deep fer me!
I want plane facts, and I want plane words,
  Of the good old-fashiond ways,
When speech run free as the songs of birds
  'Way back in the airly days.

Tell me a tale of the timber-lands—
  Of the old-time pioneers;
Somepin' a pore man understands
  With his feelins's well as ears.
Tell of the old log house,—about
  The loft, and the puncheon floor—
The old fi-er-place, with the crane swung out,
  And the latch-string through the door.

Tell of the things jest as they was—
  They don't need no excuse!—
Don't tech 'em up' like the poets does,
  Tel theyr all too fine fer use!—
Say they was 'leven in the fambily—
  Two beds, and the chist, below,
And the trundle-beds that each helt three,
  And the clock and the old bureau.

Then blow the horn at the old back-door
  Tel the echoes all halloo,
And the childern gethers home onc't more,
  Jest as they ust to do:
Blow fer Pap tel he hears and comes,
  With Tomps and Elias, too,
A-marchin' home, with the fife and drums
  And the old Red White and Blue!

Blow and blow tel the sound draps low
  As the moan of the whipperwill,
And wake up Mother, and Ruth and Jo,
  All sleepin' at Bethel Hill:
Blow and call tel the faces all
  Shine out in the back-log's blaze,
And the shadders dance on the old hewed wall
  As they did in the airly days.

"MYLO JONES'S WIFE."

"Mylo Jones's Wife" was all
I heerd, mighty near, last Fall—
Visitun relations down
Tother side of Morgantown!
Mylo Jones's wife she does
This and that, and "those" and "thus"!—
Can't 'bide babies in her sight—
Ner no childern, day and night,
Whoopin' round the premises—
Ner no nothin' else, I guess!

Mylo Jones's wife she 'lows
She's the boss of her own house!—
Mylo—consequences is—
Stays whare things seem *some* like *his*,—
Uses, mostly, with the stock—
Coaxin' "Old Kate" not to balk,
Ner kick hossflies' branes out, ner
Act, I s'pose, so much like *her!*
Yit the wimmern-folks tells you
She's *perfection*.—Yes they do!

Mylo's wife she says she's found
Home haint home with *men-folks* round,
When they's work like *hern* to do—
Picklin' pears and *butchern*, too,
And a-rendern lard, and then
Cookin fer a pack of men
To come trackin' up the floor
She's scrubbed *tel* she'll scrub no *more!*—
Yit she'd keep things clean ef they
Made her scrub tel Jedgmunt Day!

Mylo Jones's wife she sews
Carpet-rags and patches clothes
Jest year *in* and *out!*—and yit
Whare's the livin' use of it?
She asts Mylo that.—And he
Gits back whare he'd ruther be,
With his team;—jest *plows*—and don't
Never sware—like some folks wont!
Think ef *he'd cut loose*, I gum!
'D he'p his heavenly chances some!

Mylo's wife don't see no use,
Ner no reason ner excuse
Fer his pore relations to
Hang round like they allus do!

Thare 'bout onc't a year—and *she*—
She jest *ga'nts* 'em, folks tells me,
On spiced pears!—Pass Mylo one,
He says "No, he don't chuse none!"
Workin' men like Mylo they
'D ort to have *meat* ev'ry day!

Dad-burn Mylo Jones's wife!
Ruther rake a blame caseknife
'Crost my wizzen than to see
Sich a womern rulin' *me!*—
Ruther take and turn in and
Raise a fool mule-colt by hand!
Mylo, though—od-rot the man!—
Jest keeps ca'm—like some folks *can*—
And 'lows sich as her, I s'pose,
Is *Man's hepmeet*!—Mercy knows!

ON A SPLENDUD MATCH.

[On the night of the marraige of the foregoin' couple, which shall be nameless here, these lines was ca'mly dashed off in the albun of the happy bride whilse the shivver-ree was goin' on outside the residence.]

HE was warned aginst the *womern*—
She was warned aginst the *man*.—
And ef that won't make a weddin',
Wy, they's nothin' else that can!

OLD JOHN CLEVENGER ON BUCKEYES.

OLD John Clevenger lets on,
  Allus, like he's purty rough
Timber.—He's a grate old John!—
  "Rough?"—don't swaller no sich stuff!
Moved here, sence the war was through,
  From Ohio—somers near
Old Bucyrus,—loyal, too,
  As us "Hoosiers" is to *here!*
Git old John stirred up a bit
  On his old home stompin'-ground—
Talks same as he lived thare yit,
  When some subject brings it round—
Like, fer instunce, Sund'y last,
  Fetched his wife, and et and stayed
All night with us.—Set and gassed
  Tel plum midnight—'cause I made
Some remark 'bout "buckeyes" and
  "What was buckeyes good fer?"—So,
Like I 'lowed, he waved his hand
  And lit in and let me know:—

"'What is Buckeyes good fer?'—What's
Pineys and *fergitmenots*?—
Honeysuckles, and sweet-peas,
And sweet-williamsuz, and these
Johnny-jump-ups ev'rywhare,
Growin' round the roots o' trees
In Spring-weather?—what air *they*
Good fer?—kin you tell me—*Hey?*
'Good to look at?' Well they air!
'Specially when *Winter's* gone,
Clean *dead-certin!* and the wood's
Green again, and sun feels good's
June!—and shed your blame boots on
The back porch, and lit out to
Roam round like you ust to do,
Barefoot, up and down the crick,
Whare the buckeyes growed so thick,
And witch-hazel and pop-paws,
And hackberries and black-haws—
With wild pizen-vines jis knit
Over and *en-nunder* it,
And wove round it all, I jing!
Tel you couldn't hardly stick
A durn *caseknife* through the thing!
Wriggle round through *that*; and then—
All het-up, and scratched and tanned,
And muskeeter-bit and mean-

Feelin'—all at onc't again,
Come out suddent on a clean
Slopin' little hump o' green
Dry soft grass, as fine and grand
As a pollor-sofy!—And
Jis pile down thare!—and tell *me*
Anywhares you'd ruther be—
'Ceptin' *right thare*, with the wild-
Flowrs all round ye, and your eyes
Smilin' with 'em at the skies,
Happy as a little child!
Well!—right here, *I* want to say,
Poets kin talk all they please
'Bout 'wild-flowrs, in colors gay',
And 'sweet blossoms flauntin' theyr
Beauteous fragrunce on the breeze'—
But the sight o' *buckeyes* jis
Sweet to me as *blossoms* is!

"I'm *Ohio-born*—right whare
People's *all* called "Buckeyes" *thare*—
'Cause, I s'pose, our buckeye crap's
Biggest in the world, perhaps!—
Ner my head don't stretch my hat
Too much on account o' *that!*—
'Cause it's Natchur's ginerus hand
Sows 'em broadcast ore the land,

With eye-single fer man's good
And the gineral neghborhood!
So *buckeyes* jis natchurly
'Pears like *kith-and-kin* to *me!*
'Slike the good old sayin' wuz,
'Purty *is* as purty *does!*'—
We can't *eat* 'em, cooked er raw—
Yit, I mind, *tomattusuz*
Wuz considered pizenus
Onc't—and dassent eat 'em!—*Pshaw*—
'Twouldn't take *me* by supprise,
Someday, ef we et *bookeyes!*
That, though, 's nuther here ner thare!—
Jis the Buckeye, whare we air,
In the present times, is what
Ockuppies my lovin' care
And my most perfoundest thought!
...Guess, this minute, what I got
In my pocket, 'at I've packed
Purt-'nigh forty year.'—A dry,
Slick and shiny, warped and cracked,
Wilted, weazened old *buckeye!*
What's it *thare* fer? What's my hart
In my *brest* fer?—'Cause its part
Of my *life*—and 'tends to biz—
Like this *buckeye's* bound to act—
'Cause *it* 'tends to *Rhumatiz!*

"...Ketched more *rhumatiz* than *fish*,
Seinen', onc't—and pants froze on
My blame legs!—And ust to wish
I wuz well er *dead and gone!*
Doc give up the case, and shod
His old hoss again and stayed
On good roads!—*And thare I laid!*
Pap he tuck some bluegrass sod
Steeped in whisky, bilin'-hot,
And socked *that* on! Then I got
Sorto' holt o' him, *somehow*—
Kindo' crazy like, they say—
And I'd *killed* him, like as not,
Ef I hadn't swooned away!
Smell my scortcht pelt purt 'nigh now!
Well—to make a long tale short—
I hung on the blame disease
Like a shavin'-hoss! and sort
O' wore it out by slow degrees—
Tell my legs wuz straight enugh
To poke through my pants again
And kick all the doctor-stuff
In the fier-place! Then turned in
And tuck Daddy Craig's old cuore—
Jis a buckeye—and that's *shore.*—
Haint no case o' rhumatiz
Kin subsist whare buckeyes is!"

THE HOSS.

THE HOSS he is a splendud beast;
He is man's friend, as heaven designed,
And, search the world from west to east,
No honester you'll ever find!

Some calls the hoss "a pore dumb brute,"
And yit, like Him who died fer you,
I say, as I theyr charge refute,
"'Fergive; they know not what they do!'"

No wiser animal makes tracks
Upon these earthly shores, and hence
Arose the axium, true as facts,
Extolled by all, as "Good hoss-sense!"

The hoss is strong, and knows his stren'th,—
You hitch him up a time er two
And lash him, and he'll go his le'nth,
And kick the dashboard out fer you!

But, treat him allus good and kind,
And never strike him with a stick,
Ner aggervate him, and you'll find
He'll never do a hostile trick.

A hoss whose master tends him right
  And worters him with daily care,
Will do your biddin' with delight,
  And act as docile as *you* air.

He'll paw and prance to hear your praise,
  Because he's learnt to love you well;
And, though you can't tell what he says,
  He'll nicker all he wants to tell.

He knows you when you slam the gate
  At early dawn, upon your way
Unto the barn, and snorts elate,
  To git his corn, er oats, er hay.

He knows you, as the orphant knows
  The folks that loves her like theyr own,
And raises her and "finds" her clothes,
  And "schools" her tel a womern-grown!

I claim no hoss will harm a man,
  Ner kick, ner run away, cavort,
Stump-suck, er balk, er "catamaran,"
  Ef you'll jest treat him as you ort.

But when I see the beast abused,
  And clubbed around as I've saw some,
I want to see his owner noosed,
  And jest yanked up like Absolum!

Of course they's differunce in stock,—
  A hoss that has a little yeer,
And slender build, and shaller hock,
  Can beat his shadder, mighty near!

Whilse one that's thick in neck and chist
  And big in leg and full in flank,
That tries to race, I still insist
  He'll have to take the second rank.

And I have jest laid back and laughed,
  And rolled and wallered in the grass
At fairs, to see some heavy-draft
  Lead out at *first*, yit come in *last!*

Each hoss has his appinted place,—
  The heavy hoss should plow the soil;—
The blooded racer, he must race,
  And win big wages fer his toil.

I never bet—ner never wrought
  Upon my feller-man to bet—
And yit, at times, I've often thought
  Of my convictions with regret.

I bless the hoss from hoof to head—
  From head to hoof, and tale to mane!—
I bless the hoss, as I have said,
  From head to hoof, and back again!

I love my God the first of all,
  Then him that perished on the cross;
And next, my wife,—and then I fall
  Down on my knees and love the hoss.

EZRA HOUSE.

[These lines was writ, in ruther high sperits, jest at the close of what's called the Anti Bellum Days, and more to be a-foolin' than anything else,—though they is more er less facts in it. But some of the boys, at the time we was all a-singin' it, fer Ezry's benefit, to the old tune of "The Oak and the Ash and the Bonny Willer Tree," got it struck off in the weekly, without leave er lisence of mine; and so sence they's allus some of 'em left to rigg me about it yit, I might as well claim the thing right here and now, so here goes. I give it jest as it appeard, fixed up and grammatisized consider'ble, as the editer told me he took the liburty of doin', in that sturling old home paper THE ADVANCE—as sound a paper yit to-day and as stanch and abul as you'll find in a hunderd.]

COME listen, good people, while a story I do tell,
Of the sad fate of one which I knew so passing well;
He enlisted at McCordsville, to battle in the south,
And protect his country's union; his name was Ezra House.

He was a young school-teacher, and educated high
In regards to Ray's arithmetic, and also Algebra:
He give good satisfaction, but at his country's call
He dropped his position, his Algebra and all.

"Its Oh, I'm going to leave you, kind scholars," he said—
For he wrote a composition the last day and read;
And it brought many tears in the eyes of the school,
To say nothing of his sweetheart he was going to leave so
soon.

"I have many recollections to take with me away,
Of the merry transpirations in the school-room so gay;
And of all that's past and gone I will never regret
I went to serve my country at the first of the outset!"

He was a good penman, and the lines that he wrote
On that sad occasion was too fine for me to quote,—
For I was there and heard it, and I ever will recall
It brought the happy tears to the eyes of us all.

And when he left, his sweetheart she fainted away,
And said she could never forget the sad day
When her lover so noble, and gallant and gay,
Said "Fare you well, my true love!" and went marching away.

But he hadn't been gone for more than two months,
When the sad news come—"he was in a skirmish once,
And a cruel rebel ball had wounded him full sore
In the region of the chin, through the canteen he wore."

But his health recruited up, and his wounds they got well,
But whilst he was in battle at Bull Run or Malvern Hill,
The news come again, so sorrowful to hear—
"A sliver from a bombshell cut off his right ear."

But he stuck to the boys, and it's often he would write,
That "he wasn't afraid for his country to fight."
But oh, had he returned on a furlough, I believe
He would not, to-day, have such cause to grieve.

For in another battle—the name I never heard—
He was guarding the wagons when an accident occurred,—
A comrade who was under the influence of drink,
Shot him with a musket through the right cheek, I think.

But his dear life was spared; but it hadn't been for long,
'Till a cruel rebel colonel come riding along,
And struck him with his sword, as many do suppose,
For his cap-rim was cut off, and also his nose.

But Providence, who watches o'er the noble and the brave,
Snatched him once more from the jaws of the grave;
And just a little while before the close of the war,
He sent his picture home to his girl away so far.

And she fell into decline. and she wrote in reply,
"She had seen his face again and was ready to die;"
And she wanted him to promise, when she was in her tomb,
He would only visit that by the light of the moon.

But he never returned at the close of the war,
And the boys that got back said he hadn't the heart;
But he got a position in a powder-mill, and said
He hoped to meet the doom that his country denied.

A PEN-PICTUR'
OF A CERTIN FRIVVOLUS OLD MAN.

MOST ontimely old man yit!
  'Pear-like sometimes he jest *tries*
His fool-self, and takes the bitt
  In his teeth and jest de-fies
All perpryties!—Lay and swet
  Doin' *nothin'*—only jest
Sorto' speckillatun on
Whare old summertimes is gone,
  And 'bout things that he loved best
When a youngster! Heerd him say
Springtimes made him thataway—
  Speshully on *Sund'ys*—when
  Sun shines out and in again,
And the lonesome old hens they
  Git off under the old kern-
  Bushes, and in deep concern
Talk-like to theyrselvs, and scratch
  Kindo' absunt-minded, jest
Like theyr thoughts was fur away
In some neghbor's gyarden-patch
  Folks has tended carefullest!

Heerd the old man dwell on these
  Idys time and time again!—
Heerd him claim that orchurd-trees
  Bloomin', put the mischief in
His old hart sometimes that bad
And owdacious that he "*had*
  To break loose *some*way," says he,
  "Ornry as I ust to be!"

Heerd him say one time—when I
Was a sorto' standin' by,
  And the air so still and clear,
  Heerd the bell fer church clean here!—
Said: "Ef I could climb and set
  On the old three-cornerd rail
Old home-place, nigh Maryette',
  Swop my soul off, hide and tale!"
And-sir! blame ef tear and laugh
Didn't ketch him half and half!
  "Oh!" he says, "to wake and be
Barefoot, in the airly dawn
  In the pastur!—thare," says he,
"Standin' whare the cow's slep' on
  The cold, dewy grass that's got
  Print of her jest steamy hot
Fer to warm a feller's heels
In a while!—How good it feels!

Sund'y!—Country!—Morning!—Hear
Nothin' but the *siluncc.*—see
Nothin' but green woods and clear
Skies and unwrit poetry
By the acre!...Oh!" says he,
"What's this voice of mine?—to seek
To speak out, and yit *can't* speak!

"*Think!*—the lazyest of days"—
Takin' his contrairyest leap,
He went on,—"git up, er sleep—
Er whilse feedin', watch the haze
Dancin' 'crost the wheat,—and keep
My pipe goin' laisurely—
Puff and whiff as pleases me,—
Er I'll leave a trail of smoke
Through *the house!*—no one'll say
'*Throw that nasty thing away!*'
'Pear-like nothin' sacerd's broke,
Goin' barefoot ef I chuse!—
I *have fiddled;*—and dug bait
And *went fishin';*—pitched hoss-shoes—
Whare they couldn't see us from
The main road.—And I've *beat* some.
I've set round and had my joke
With the thrashers at the barn—
And I've swopped 'em yarn fer yarn!—

Er I've hepped the childern poke
Fer hens'-nests.—agged on a match
Twixt the boys, to watch 'em scratch
And paw round and rip and tear,
And bust buttons and pull hair
To theyr rompin' harts' content—
And me jest a-settin' thare
Hatchin' out more devilment!

"What you s'pose now ort to be
Done with sich a man?" says he—
"Sich a fool-old-man as me!"

WET-WEATHER TALK.

It hain't no use to grumble and complane;
  It's jest as cheap and easy to rejoice;
When God sorts out the weather and sends rain,
    W'y, rain's my choice.

Men giner'ly, to all intents—
  Although they're apt to grumble some—
Puts most theyr trust in Providence,
  And takes things as they come—
    That is, the commonality
    Of men that's lived as long as me
    Has watched the world enugh to learn
    They're not the boss of this concern.

With *some*, of course, it's different—
  I've saw *young* men that knowed it all,
And didn't like the way things went
  On this terrestial ball;—
    But all the same, the rain, some way,
    Rained jest as hard on picnic day;
    Er, when they railly *wanted* it,
    It mayby wouldn't rain a bit!

In this existunce, dry and wet
  Will overtake the best of men—
Some little skift o' clouds'll shet
  The sun off now and then.—
    And mayby, whilse you're wundern who
    You've fool-like lent your umbrell' to,
    And *want* it—out'll pop the sun,
    And you'll be glad you hain't got none!

It aggervates the farmers, too—
  They's too much wet, er too much sun,
Er work, er waitin' round to do
  Before the plowin's done.
    And mayby, like as not, the wheat,
    Jest as it's lookin' hard to beat,
    Will ketch the storm—and jest about
    The time the corn's a-jintin' out.

These-here *cy-clones* a-foolin' round—
  And back'ard crops!—and wind and rain!—
And yit the corn that's wallerd down
  May elbow up again!—
    They hain't no sense, as I can see,
    Fer mortuls, sich as us, to be
    A-faultin' Natchur's wise intents,
    And lockin' horns with Providence!

It hain't no use to grumble and complane;
  Its jest as cheap and easy to rejoice.—
When God sorts out the weather and sends rain,
    W'y, rain's my choice.

THOUGHTS ON A PORE JOKE.

I like fun—and I like jokes
'Bout as well as most o' folks!—
  Like my joke, and like my fun;—
But a joke, I'll state right here,
'S got some p'int—er I don't keer
  Fer no joke that haint got none.—
I haint got no use, I'll say,
Fer a *pore* joke, anyway!

F'rinstunce, now, when *some* folks gits
To relyin' on theyr wits,
Ten to one they git too smart
And *spile* it all, right at the start!
  Feller wants to jest go slow
  And do his *thinkin'* first, you know.
'F I can't think up somepin' good,
I set still and chaw my cood!
  'F you *think* nothin'—jest keep on,
  But don't *say* it—er you're gone!

A MORTUL PRAYER.

OH! Thou that vaileth from all eyes
  The glory of thy face,
And setteth throned behind the skies
  In thy abiding-place:
Though I but dimly reco'nize
  Thy purposes of grace;
And though with weak and wavering
  Deserts, and vexd with fears,
I lift the hands I cannot wring
  All dry of sorrow's tears,
Make puore my prayers that daily wing
  Theyr way unto thy ears!

Oh! with the hand that tames the flood
  And smooths the storm to rest,
Make bammy dews of all the blood
  That stormeth in my brest,
And so refresh my hart to bud
  And bloom the loveliest.
Lull all the clammer of my soul
  To silunce; bring release
Unto the brane still in controle
  Of doubts; bid sin to cease,
And let the waves of pashun roll
  And kiss the shores of peace.

Make me to love my feller-man—
  Yea, though his bitterness
Doth bite as only adders can—
  Let *me* the fault confess,
And go to him and clasp his hand
  And love him none the less.
So keep me, Lord, ferever free
  From vane concete er whim;
And he whose pius eyes can see
  My faults, however dim,—
Oh! let him pray the least fer me,
  And me the most fer him.

THE FIRST BLUEBIRD.

JEST rain and snow! and rain again!
  And dribble! drip! and blow!
Then snow! and thaw! and slush! and then—
  Some more rain and snow!

This morning I was 'most afeard
  To *wake* up—when, I jing!
I seen the sun shine out and heerd
  The first bluebird of Spring!—
Mother she'd raised the winder some;—
And in acrost the orchurd come,
  Soft as a angel's wing,
A breezy, treesy, beesy hum,
  Too sweet fer anything!

The winter's shroud was rent a-part—
  The sun bust forth in glee,—
And when *that bluebird* sung, my hart
  Hopped out o' bed with me!

EVAGENE BAKER—WHO WAS DYIN OF DRED GONSUMTION AS THESE LINES WAS PENNED BY A TRUE FRIEND.

Pore afflicted Evagene!
Whilse the woods is fresh and green,
And the birds on ev'ry hand
Sings in rapture sweet and grand,—
Thou, of all the joyus train,
Art bedridden, and in pain
  Sich as only them can cherish
  Who, like flowrs, is first to perish!

When the neghbors brought the word
She was down the folks inferred
It was jest a cold she'd caught,
Dressin' thinner than she'd ort
Fer the frolicks and the fun
Of the dancin' that she'd done
  'Fore the Spring was flush er ary
  Blossom on the peach er cherry.

But, last Sund'y, her request
Fer the Church's prayers was jest
Rail hart-renderin' to hear!—
Many was the silunt tear
And the tremblin' sigh, to show
She was dear to us below
  On this earth—and *dearer*, even,
  When we thought of her a-leavin'!

Sisters prayed, and coted from
Genesis to Kingdom-come
Provin' of her title clear
To the mansions.—"Even *her*,"
They claimed, "might be saved, *someway*,
Though she'd danced and played crowkay,
  And wrought on her folks to git her
  Fancy shoes that never fit her!"

Us to pray fer *Evagene!*—
With her hart as puore and clean
As a rose is after rain
When the sun comes out again!—
What's the use to pray fer *her?*
She don't need no prayin' fer!—
  Needed, all her life, more *playin'*
  Than she ever needed prayin'!

I jest thought of all she'd been
Sence her *mother* died, and when
She turned in and done *her* part—
All *her* cares on that child-hart!—
Thought of years she'd slaved—and had
Saved the farm—danced and was glad...
  Mayby Him who marks the sporry
  Will smooth down her wings tomorry!

ON ANY ORDENARY MAN IN A HIGH STATE OF LAUGHTURE AND DELIGHT.

As its give' me to percieve,
I most certin'y believe
When a man's jest glad plum through,
God's pleased with him, same as you.

TOWN AND COUNTRY.

They's a predjudice allus twixt country and town
  Which I wisht in my hart wasent so.
You take *city* people, jest square up and down,
  And theyr mighty good people to know:
And whare's better people a-livin', to-day,
  Than us in the *country*?—Yit good
As both of us is, we're divorsed, you might say,
  And won't compermise when we could!

Now as nigh into town fer yer Pap, ef you please,
  Is the what's called the sooburbs.—Fer thare
You'll at least ketch a whiff of the breeze and a sniff
  Of the breth of wild-flowrs ev'rywhare.
They's room fer the childern to play, and grow, too—
  And to roll in the grass, er to climb
Up a tree and rob nests, like they *ortent* to do,
  But they'll do *any*how ev'ry time!

My Son-in-law said, when he lived in the town,
  He jest natchurly pined, night and day,
Fer a sight of the woods, er a acre of ground
  Whare the trees wasent all cleared away!

And he says to me onc't, whilse a-visitin' us
On the farm, "It's not strange, I declare,
That we can't coax you folks, without raisin' a fuss,
To come to town, visitin' thare!"

And says I, "Then git back whare you sorto' *belong*—
And *Madaline*, too,—and yer three
Little childern," says I, "that don't know a bird-song,
Ner a hawk from a chicky-dee-dee!
Git back," I-says-I, "to the blue of the sky
And the green of the fields, and the shine
Of the sun, with a laugh in yer voice and yer eye
As harty as Mother's and mine!"

Well—long-and-short of it,—he's compermised *some*—
He's moved in the sooburbs.—And now
They don't haf to coax, when they want us to come,
'Cause we turn in and go *anyhow!*
Fer thare—well, they's room fer the songs and purfume
Of the grove and the old orchurd-ground,
And they's room fer the childern out thare, and they's room
Fer theyr Gran' pap to waller 'em round!

LINES FER ISAAC BRADWELL, OF INDANOPLIS, IND., COUNTY-SEAT OF MARION.

[Writ on the flyleaf of a volume of the author's poems that come in one of gittin' burnt up in the great Bowen-Merrill's fire of March 17, 1890.]

THROUGH fire and flood this book has passed.—
Fer what?—I hardly dare to ast—
Less'n its still to pamper me
With extry food fer vanity;—
Fer, sence its fell in hands as true
As *yourn* is— and a *Hoosier* too,—
I'm prouder of the book, I jing!
Than 'fore they tried to burn the thing!

DECORATION DAY ON THE PLACE.

ITS LONESOME—sorto' lonesome,—its a *Sund'y-day*, to me,
It 'pears-like—more'n any day I nearly ever see!
Yit, with the Stars and Stripes above, a-flutterin' in the air,
On ev'ry Soldier's grave I'd love to lay a lilly thare.

They say, though, Decoration Days is ginerly observed
'Most *ev'rywhares*—espeshally by soldier-boys that's served.—
But me and Mother's never went—we seldom git away,—
In pint o' fact, we're *allus* home on *Decoration Day.*

They say the old boys marches through the streets in colum's grand,
A-follerin' the old war-tunes theyr playin' on the band—
And citizuns all jinin' in—and little childern, too—
All marchin', under shelter of the old Red White and Blue.—

With roses! roses! roses!—ev'rybody in the town!—
And crowds o' little girls in white, jest fairly loaded down!—
Oh! don't THE BOYS know it, from theyr camp acrost the hill?—
Don't they see theyr com'ards comin' and the old flag wavin' still?

Oh! can't they hear the bugul and the rattle of the drum?—
Ain't they no way under heavens they can rickollect us some?
Ain't they no way we can coax 'em, through the roses, jest to say
They know that ev'ry day on earth's theyr Decoration Day?

We've tried that—me and Mother,—whare Elias takes his rest,
In the orchurd—in his uniform, and hands acrost his brest,
And the flag he died fer, smilin' and a-ripplin' in the breeze
Above his grave—and over that,—*the robin in the trees!*

And *yit* its lonesome—lonesome!—It's a *Sund'y-day*, to *me*,
It 'pears-like—more'n any day I nearly ever see!—
Still, with the Stars and Stripes above, a-flutterin' in the air,
On ev'ry Soldier's grave I'd love to lay a lilly thare.

www.ingramcontent.com/pod-product-compliance
Lightning Source LLC
LaVergne TN
LVHW021424110826
845150LV00007B/2077